*We know much
about the mountains and oceans of Earth,
spinning with us
around the flaring Sun.*

*We know something
of the space in between,
where swift Mercury and sizzling Venus track our sky.*

We've become familiar
with our closest neighbors—
the cratered moon, desert-red Mars, and the rubble of asteroids,

*We've swooped by
Jupiter's swirling storm, Saturn's chunky ringlets,
and crowds of circling moons.*

We've sped past
sideways Uranus and windy Neptune,
skirting the outer reaches of our solar system.

But we want to go farther.
We long to explore.
To know even more.

We dream of discovering what lies . . .

BEYOND

DISCOVERIES FROM THE OUTER REACHES OF SPACE

MIRANDA PAUL

ILLUSTRATED BY SIJA HONG

Millbrook Press / Minneapolis

The frigid glitter of a trillion comets
zooms in a cosmic ring.
Dwarf planets with tiny moons and atmospheres that freeze and fall
bring action and excitement.
Hang on—we haven't even left the neighborhood.

PAST THE PLANETS:
KUIPER BELT
29-49 AU
(~3-5 billion miles)
from Earth

A swarm of icy bodies—some as big as mountains—
forms a cloudy border around our cosmic village.
It's so mysterious we've never seen it,
like a snowy fog covering our distant, traveling neighbor.
But when traffic gets heavy, we can't miss the drama:
watch these dirty snowballs come hurtling toward our sun.

AT THE EDGE:
OORT CLOUD
5,000-100,000 AU
(~464 billion - 929 trillion miles /
0.79 - 1.6 light-years)
from Earth

*Round exoplanets appear in the
scopes of our sensors:
Wind-whipped worlds with
endless days and nights.
Dark realms where gemstones
fall from the sky.*

**4.25 light-years
from Earth
Proxima b—tidally locked
into half day/half night**

**1,043 light-years
from Earth
HAP-P-7b—a dark realm
that might rain rubies
and sapphires**

Earth-like planets with
twilight skies.
Giant spheres of scorching gas
speeding in their orbits.

~500 light-years
from Earth
Kepler-186f—an Earth-like
planet with twilight skies

200 light-years
from Earth
Kepler-16b—a world
with two suns

190 light-years
from Earth
HD 80606 b—a giant,
scorching sphere
of gas

Horizons with two setting suns.

Are these fantastical places real?
Yes, yes, yes.
But a thousand answers
spark a million new questions.

A white pinprick burns at the center
of a glowing, glaring eyeball of ash.
Radiation, heat, and dust make the show spectacular.

Death.

MILKY WAY:
INTERSTELLAR NEIGHBORHOOD
HELIX NEBULA (a dying star)
~650 light-years
from Earth

MILKY WAY:
INTERSTELLAR NEIGHBORHOOD
ORION NEBULA (a star
birthplace)
~1,300 light-years
from Earth

Within a galactic arm,
a trapezoid of precious sky jewels shines.
Enormous clouds squeeze together
with tremendous heat
and crushing pressure.
Puffs of clouds break away,
stoking the cosmic fire of creation—
a star-forming, stellar nursery.

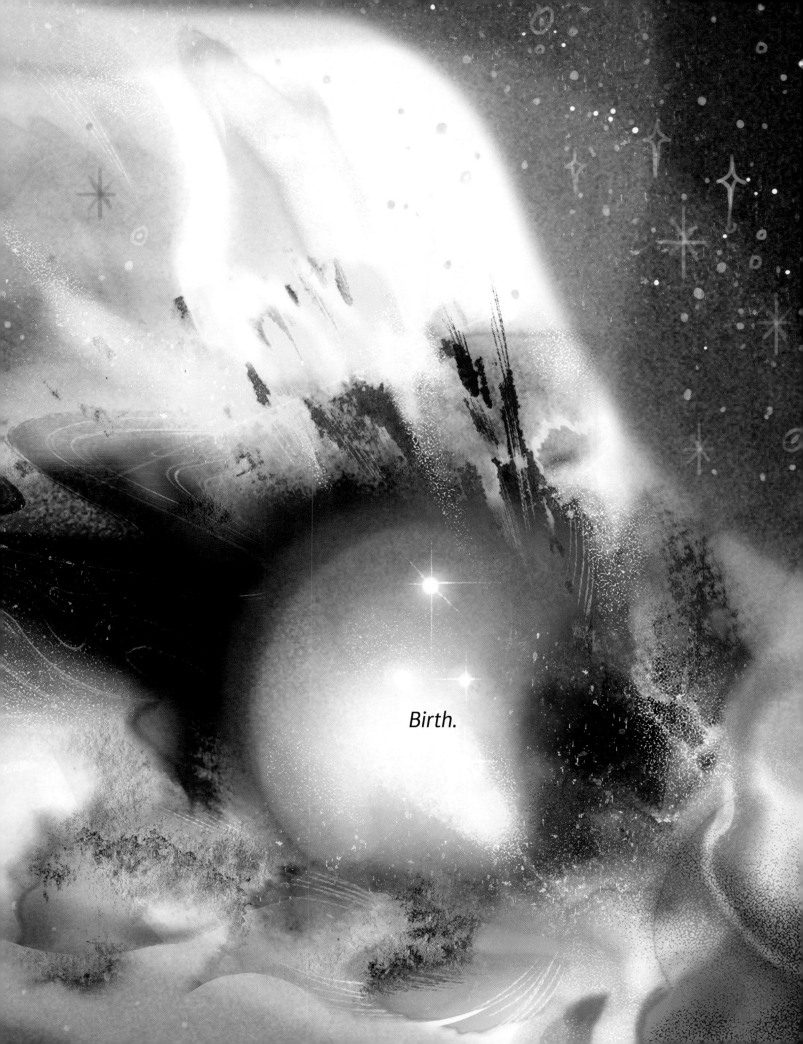

Birth.

Heavy and dark,
the black hole in the center of our galaxy
is a risky playground—
flashing echoes of light,
giving forth radio signals,
sending swirls of gas spinning like a supersonic merry-go-round.

Jets rocket above and below, rides for extreme adventurers.
Looking for the ultimate event? Step right up toward its supermassive core,
which swallows anything that dares to swing
too close to its harsh domain.

Enjoy the ride!

*The farther you go, the closer something becomes:
darkness.*

*The vast distances and powerful emptiness
are so common out here,
every other actual thing
becomes rare.*

OUTSIDE THE
MILKY WAY GALAXY:
LOCAL GROUP
~65 million light-years
from Earth

VIRGO SUPERCLUSTER
110 million light-years
in diameter

Thousands of swirls and spirals
have already accepted their invitation to this thirteen-billion-year-old campfire.
Dark matter lures the speckled crowd like an intergalactic host.
Chains of light form links and clumps against the charcoal emptiness.
Illuminated butterflies interlace their starry wings.

But is this fireside gathering haunted?
A strange energy lurks like a ghost between the guests—
an invisible decoration?
Other parties pale in comparison.

Stretching the limits
of what we can detect
(but not what we can imagine),
a colossal, expanding horizon guards the great beyond.
The vastness whispers,
"You are small . . .

*"but the adventures that await you
are infinite."*

BEYOND THE POEMS
More Information about the Places in Our Cosmic Neighborhood

Frigid glitter . . . atmospheres that freeze and fall: The Kuiper Belt, where dwarf planets (including Pluto) and comets reside, is a doughnut-shaped ring that contains hundreds of thousands of icy bodies believed to be remnants from the formation of the solar system. Artists' drawings of the Kuiper Belt depict this area as a glittery or powdered-sugary *O*. As of the day this was written, more than two thousand Kuiper Belt objects, or KBOs, have been observed and recorded, but there are also small rocks as well as trillions of comets temporarily traveling through this area. Some of the KBOs now known as dwarf planets have very thin air, and their atmospheres freeze and collapse when they orbit too far from the Sun. Many of them also have their own moons. NASA's *New Horizons* was the first spacecraft to actually visit an object in the Kuiper Belt when it flew past Pluto in July 2015. On January 1, 2019, it passed by the farthest solar system object we've ever observed, a fossil-like rock called Ultima Thule, which scientist Alan Stern said "looks like a snowman."

Cloudy border . . . dirty snowballs come hurtling: Unlike the Kuiper Belt, which is a ring, the Oort cloud is like a giant bubble of large and small objects that forms a border around the whole solar system. Although it's often listed as the next thing in our "neighborhood" after the Kuiper Belt, it's more than one hundred times farther away. That means it will take three hundred years before *Voyager 1*—a space probe humans launched in 1977 to study the outer solar system—reaches it! Scientists believe the mountain-sized objects in the Oort cloud orbit in all different directions. Every once in a while, when something disturbs the orbit of an icy body from the Oort cloud, it starts to fall inward, sometimes disintegrating if it comes too close to the Sun. A comet nicknamed Siding Spring actually hurtled past Mars in 2014, disrupting its magnetic field and causing a meteor shower—major drama! Luckily for the Red Planet, this comet will not return for about 740,000 years.

Round exoplanets: Exoplanets are worlds that orbit around other stars besides the Sun. Since these planets are too far away for us to see, NASA launched a space telescope called Kepler to detect these worlds. Kepler allows us to use the transit method to detect planets—which involves observing the shadow of a planet passing in front of a star. (There are other ways we can detect exoplanets too.) More than 4,150 exoplanets in the Milky Way had already been detected and catalogued by the time this sentence was printed. A 2018 study suggests that there may be even more exoplanets outside of our Milky Way galaxy. What we've found has surprised many scientists—planets with lava oceans, multiple suns, and other fantasylike features such as clouds that rain rubies and sapphires. Although it's fun to imagine traveling to these worlds, they're too far away to get to—and if we ever got there, we might find out that they're not actually suitable to live on!

Glowing, glaring eyeball: The Helix Nebula is a dying star that humans can spot by looking toward the constellation Aquarius. When a star like this dies, it "throws a tantrum" (according to NASA), tossing and turning anything in its orbit about as the dust of its outer layers burps into space. This particular star has become a white dwarf—about the size of Earth—whose hot core is glowing with extreme ultraviolet radiation (the waves that give you sunburn). These kinds of nebulae looked like planets to early scientists, so they were called planetary nebulae, but they don't birth planets. Eventually, all that will be left of the star is its very heavy core. A single teaspoon of a white dwarf could weigh as much or more than a *Tyrannosaurus rex*. Now that's a massive goodbye!

Trapezoid of precious sky jewels . . . birth: The Orion Nebula is Earth's closest large star-forming region, and it is the brightest in the Northern Hemisphere sky. It can be spotted with the naked eye or observed with a handheld telescope (January is the best time to look for it). The nebula gives birth to huge numbers of stars, but it is marked by four of its brightest stellar creations that form a trapezoid shape and shine like diamonds in Hubble Space Telescope images.

The black hole in the center of our galaxy: The center of the Milky Way is home to a black hole called Sagittarius A* (whose signals appear from Earth to be coming from beyond the stars of a constellation known as Sagittarius). A black hole isn't really a hole, though. It often begins as a dead star or stellar collision and becomes a super-packed dark object with incredible gravity that pulls in whatever comes too close. Around it, extreme forces cause debris in the area to sizzle hot, which sends out X-rays and gamma rays and forms bright jets of particles that can shoot hundreds of thousands of light-years into space! In 2019 scientists captured an image of a black hole and its shadow for the first time using the Event Horizon Telescope, which is actually an international network of radio telescopes. (The black hole they imaged is in the Messier 87 galaxy).

The vast distances and powerful emptiness: With a name like the Local Group, you might think that the thirty galaxies nearest to our solar system are like houses on the same block with their porch lights on. Compared to how vast the universe is, they are relatively close, like neighbors. However, in terms of space, the reality is that *nothing* is close together. Most of space is dark, with long distances (that take hundreds and thousands and millions of Earth years) to reach. Not all of the darkness is completely empty, though. Bits of dust and ice and gas move about in small quantities, and larger bodies (such as comets and planets) are sometimes flung out of orbits and become rogue. These objects on the move are important because their atoms can become the atoms of living and nonliving things wherever they land!

Illuminated butterflies . . . strange energy: Scientists estimate that the Virgo Supercluster has twenty thousand or more galaxies, including some with remarkable shapes like the Butterfly Galaxies (NGC 4567 and NGC 4568). Although that large number may lead us to believe that space is filled with light, the Virgo Supercluster is so vast (55 million light-years from center to edge) that the dark space far exceeds the spaces with light from galaxies. Dark matter, a mysterious thing that's nearly impossible to detect, seems to have a gravitational force that draws the Milky Way and thousands of other galaxies toward one another—as though they're all traveling to a big party—and that's why they clump or cluster together. There is a second kind of darkness that is even more strange and mysterious to scientists, called dark energy. As of the time this book was written, more questions than answers exist about what dark energy is and how it operates. Maybe you'll be one of the curious minds to unlock a clue about how to measure or interact with it!

A colossal, expanding horizon: We call the whole universe—well, the part we can detect—the observable universe. To our instruments, it appears like a round horizon, and wherever we measure from is the center point. Scientists don't know for certain the exact shape of the universe, and even if we did, they've discovered it would is hard to describe the shape using three-dimensional models. It's also difficult to determine the shape of something so huge when we're so tiny and looking from the inside. By our best calculations, there are about a hundred billion galaxies in the observable universe! If you think that's big, some scientists theorize that our universe may just be Universe 1 in a larger multiverse. Among all the exciting unknowns, we do know that the universe is expanding (and has been expanding since the beginning), much as our knowledge and the possibility of future discoveries are expanding.

AUTHOR'S NOTE

When I was in fourth grade, our class learned about the solar system—from the Sun to Pluto (Pluto was still considered an official planet back then). Our textbook had bright, artistic photos and drawings of these planets. But it was a tiny asterisk (*) that caught my nine-year-old eye. The asterisk marked a line of bonus information at the bottom of the page. This short sentence informed readers that because the outer planets didn't move in perfect circles, Neptune was actually farther from the Sun than Pluto from 1979 to 1999. Suddenly, I realized that the foam ball models we'd made were technically out of order. I wondered why neat facts like this one were printed so small, surely overlooked by almost everyone. I wanted to know what other kinds of new information scientists had discovered about outer space that might not be in our textbooks at all. Where could I learn more about space? Why did most of the kids' books in my school's library include only our solar system, beginning with the Sun and ending with Pluto? What was out there, beyond our slice of the universe?

Even before 1990, scientists had made remarkable discoveries that demonstrated just how small we actually are, and how incredibly vast the universe is, but my school's textbooks hadn't caught up. Now we know our rough cosmic address, or where (approximately) in the universe we live, and we have sent a space probe that has officially left our solar system and is now traveling in interstellar space. Scientists have also located planets outside of our solar system, called exoplanets, and some of them might be capable of supporting life. It's a fascinating time to be a space enthusiast!

Many children, including my own, love to explore. They want to discover a new species or be the first to find and share a little-known fact. While much of the land on Earth has been charted and mapped, space remains a giant mystery. Interstellar space offers scientists and citizens alike more than ample opportunities to dream, discover, and make significant contributions toward humanity's knowledge. It is my hope that this book ignites an urge to explore as it poetically celebrates our awe-inspiring cosmos. May the words I've written here honor the underappreciated endeavors of scientists and mathematicians focused on our universal frontier.

ILLUSTRATOR'S NOTE

I've often said that if I hadn't decided to become an illustrator, I definitely would have been an astronaut. Although it may sound improbable, other than drawing, the universe and astronomy are the fields that interest me most. So when I was asked to illustrate this book, it felt like a dream come true.

As I first read the manuscript, I was astonished that the universe could be presented in such a poetic and dreamlike way. Miranda took me from a spot on Earth to the vast, endless universe where I was surrounded only by silent planets. Her text led me to use a brand-new method to illustrate the book. I wanted to fill the pages with the natural, varying light of galaxies and to let every planet be embraced by soft colors and lights. It was a great challenge for me, but the process was filled with passion and joy.

Before creating the artwork, I spent a lot of time researching so that I had a good understanding of everything mentioned in the book. I also took the opportunity to visit NASA as well as the Smithsonian's National Air and Space Museum in Washington, DC. After these visits, I felt I was one step closer to the universe. Additionally, the following documentaries were especially helpful: *Cosmos: A Spacetime Odyssey*, *The Planets*, *Wonders of the Universe*, and *Journey to the Edge of the Universe*. While researching, I was filled with so much excitement for this book that everything else felt boring!

My goal with this artwork was to bring together fact and feeling, and I think I have accomplished this. I hope everyone who encounters this book has the feeling of being transported away from Earth and into the universe, just as I did. Remember, the universe is all around us—and much closer than you might think!

OUR COSMIC ADDRESS

Space is so vast that it can be hard to imagine just how far apart objects are. And to further complicate matters, the same unit of measurement doesn't work well for expressing all distances. The smallest distance in this book is given miles and astronomical units (AU). Think of it this way: 1 mile is about how far a car driving on the highway can travel in 1 minute. And 1 AU is the distance from the Sun to Earth, which is about 93 million miles. When distances get even larger, you'll see them given in light-years. A light-year is the distance light can travel in 1 year. One light-year is equal to 63,241.1 AU, which is about 6 trillion miles. The ~ symbol that comes before some numbers indicates that the number is an approximation. Because the distances are so large, objects in this book are not to scale. To accurately show all the empty space between objects would require an enormous book!

Here's another way to think about it: when we send a letter here on Earth, we might include our street name; house, apartment, or box number; city; state; and country on the envelope. These specific details give mail carriers enough information to deliver a letter. But if we were sending an interstellar message to the outer reaches of the universe, the return address might look something like this:

B. A. Voyager
123 Sunshine Circle
Star City, WI, 54321
United States
Planet Earth
The Solar System
Orion Arm, Milky Way
Local Group
Virgo Cluster
Virgo Supercluster
Laniakea Supercluster
Observable Universe (number 1?)

Future Friend
Any World, Observable Universe

Depending on where in this book you plan to send the letter, here's how long it would take to get there from Earth, assuming that SpaceMail travels at the speed of light (about 671 million miles per hour):

Sun = about 8 minutes
Jupiter = about 43 minutes
Kuiper Belt = 7 to 8 hours
closest edges of the Oort cloud = 2 to 4 weeks
farthest edges of the Oort cloud = 1.5 to 3.5 years
Proxima b = 4.25 years
55 Cancri e = 40 years

Kepler-16b = 200 years
Kepler-186f = 500 years
Helix Nebula = 650 years
Orion Nebula = 1,300 years
Sagittarius A* (black hole) = 25,000 years
outside the Milky Way = 65 million years to 93 billion years

Fine print: All times are estimated and/or rounded for ease of understanding. SpaceMail offers no guaranteed deliveries or refunds in the case of an anomaly!

EXPLORE BEYOND THIS BOOK

Books

Fishman, Seth. *A Hundred Billion Trillion Stars*. Illustrated by Isabel Greenberg. New York: Greenwillow Books, 2017.

Hughes, Catherine D. *First Big Book of Space*. Illustrated by David A. Aguilar. Washington, DC: National Geographic, 2012.

Kenney, Karen Latchana. *Exoplanets: Worlds beyond our Solar System*. Minneapolis: Twenty-First Century Books, 2017.

Manley, Curtis. *Just Right: Searching for the Goldilocks Planet*. Illustrated by Jessica Lanan. New York: Roaring Brook, 2019.

Prinja, Raman. *Planetarium*. Illustrated by Chris Wormell. Somerville, MA: Big Picture, 2018.

Websites

Exoplanet Travel Bureau
https://exoplanets.nasa.gov/alien-worlds/exoplanet-travel-bureau/
Check out posters and 360-degree simulated views of other worlds.

The Habitable Exoplanets Catalog
http://phl.upr.edu/projects/habitable-exoplanets-catalog
See artists' renditions and searchable data tables of confirmed exoplanets.

Passport to Space
https://kids.nationalgeographic.com/explore/space/passport-to-space/
This site includes space facts, photos, videos, books, and games.

Planet Hunters TESS
https://www.zooniverse.org/projects/nora-dot-eisner/planet-hunters-tess/
Join the citizen science search for undiscovered worlds.

NASA SpacePlaceExplore Earth and Space
https://spaceplace.nasa.gov/
Explore Earth and space.

Videos

The Farthest: Voyager in Space. San Francisco: PBS, 2020.

"Let's Explore Space! | Astronomy for Kids," YouTube video, 0:53. Posted by SciShowKids, June 27, 2017. https://www.youtube.com/watch?v=_QwaUmDbnGg.

"Our Milky Way Galaxy: How Big is Space?" YouTube video, 1:46. Posted by NASASolarSystem, April 2, 2019. https://www.youtube.com/watch?v=MX3PIkbTQwQ.

"Star Size Comparison 2." YouTube video, 6:50. Posted by "morn1415," August 1, 2016. https://www.youtube.com/watch?v=GoW8Tf7hTGA.

SELECTED BIBLIOGRAPHY

Admin. "Virgo Cluster." Messier Objects. August 9, 2017. http://www.messier-objects.com/virgo-cluster.

Armstrong, David J., Ernst de Mooij, Joanna Barstow, Hugh P. Osborn, James Blake, and Nessa Fereshteh Saniee. "Variability in the Atmosphere of the Hot Giant Planet HAT-P-7 b." Available online at Cornell University, December 13, 2016. arXiv:1612.04225.

"Astronomers Find Newborn Stars at the Edge of the Galaxy." Royal Astronomical Society. Accessed February 1, 2019. https://www.ras.org.uk/news-and-press/2592-astronomers-find-newborn-stars-at-the-edge-of-the-galaxy (article no longer available online).

"Black Hole Bounty Captured in the Center of the Milky Way." NASA, June 19, 2020. https://www.nasa.gov/image-feature /black-hole-bounty-captured-in-the-center-of-the-milky-way.

"Charting the Milky Way from the Inside Out." NASA. Last modified August 7, 2017. https://www.nasa.gov/jpl/charting -the-milky-way-from-the-inside-out.

Dai, Xinyu, and Eduardo Guerras. "Probing Extragalactic Planets Using Quasar Microlensing." *Astrophysical Journal Letters*, February 2, 2018. http://iopscience.iop.org/article/10.3847/2041-8213/aaa5fb.

"Dark Energy, Dark Matter." NASA. Accessed July 3, 2020. https://science.nasa.gov/astrophysics/focus-areas/what-is -dark-energy.

"Helix Nebula: Unraveling at the Seams." NASA. Last modified August 7, 2017. https://www.nasa.gov/multimedia /imagegallery/image_feature_2368.html.

"Hubble's Slice of Sagittarius." NASA. Last modified August 6, 2017. https://www.nasa.gov/image-feature/goddard /2017/hubbles-slice-of-sagittarius.

Hulbert, Melissa. "Discovering Our Cosmic Address." Museum of Applied Arts & Sciences, May 1, 2016. https://maas.museum /observations/2016/05/01/discovering-our-cosmic-address.

Mack, Eric. "Two Earth-Like Exoplanets Now Even Better Spots to Look for Life." CNet, June 29, 2018. https://www.cnet.com /news/earth-size-planets-kepler-186f-62f-now-even-better-spots-to-look-for-life.

"Messier 42 (the Orion Nebula)." NASA. Last modified December 2, 2019. https://www.nasa.gov/feature/goddard /2017/messier-42-the-orion-nebula.

Roques, Françoise, ed. "Catalog." Extrasolar Planet Encyclopaedia. Exoplanet team, Observatoire de Paris. Accessed July 6, 2020. http://exoplanet.eu/catalog.

Smale, Alan. "Imagine the Universe: The Cosmic Distance Scale; Local Group." NASA. Accessed May 22, 2019. https:// imagine.gsfc.nasa.gov/features/cosmic/local_group_info.html.

"Solar System Exploration." NASA. Accessed July 6, 2020. https://solarsystem.nasa.gov/planets/overview.

Summers, Michael E., and James Trefil. *Exoplanets: Diamonds Worlds, Super-Earths, Pulsar Planets, and the New Search for Life beyond Our Solar System.* Washington, DC: Smithsonian Books, 2017.

"Supermassive Black Hole Sagittarius A*." NASA. Last updated August 7, 2017. https://www.nasa.gov/mission_pages /chandra/multimedia/black-hole-SagittariusA.html.

Tyson, Neil deGrasse. *Astrophysics for People in a Hurry.* New York; London: W. W. Norton, 2017.

University of Warwick. "Winds of Rubies and Sapphires Strike the Sky of Giant Planet." NASA Exoplanet Exploration. December 11, 2016. https://exoplanets.nasa.gov/news/1397/winds-of-rubies-and-sapphires-strike-the-sky-of-giant-planet.

"What Lurks in the Outer Solar System?" NASA. September 13, 2001. https://science.nasa.gov/science-news/science-at-nasa /2001/ast13sep_1.

Zachos, Elaina. "More Than a Trillion Planets Could Exist beyond Our Galaxy." *National Geographic*, February 5, 2018. https://www.nationalgeographic.com/news/2018/02/exoplanets-discovery-milky-way-galaxy-spd/.

ACKNOWLEDGMENTS

A special thank-you to Christian Ready, Dr. Mike Brotherton, Adam Meyers, and Dr. Jim Verley for hosting and instructing me at Launch Pad Astronomy Workshop at the University of Wyoming while I was finishing the research for this book. Further acknowledgment goes to Chris McKitterick and Quinton Singer for reviewing the text for accuracy and clarity. Explaining these massive concepts and phenomenal discoveries of contemporary astronomy and astrophysics to young people is no small feat, and you've been nothing short of stellar in helping me comprehend a few of the incredible wonders of our observable universe. A special thank-you to Ramutis V. Kiparskis for reigniting my interest in interstellar space, which ultimately led to this book. Further acknowledgment goes to the staff and volunteers at all museums, planetariums, and observatories around the world, especially the National Air and Space Museum, the American Museum of Natural History, the Barlow Planetarium, and the Griffith, Lowell, and Wyoming Infrared Observatories, which I visited in person while writing *Beyond*.

FOR MY UNCLE CHRIS, WHO INSPIRED ME TO LEARN
AND EXPLORE BEYOND WHAT I WAS TAUGHT —M.P.

FOR MY PARENTS AND LITTLE ME —S.H.

Millbrook Press™
An imprint of Lerner Publishing Group, Inc.
241 First Avenue North
Minneapolis, MN 55401 USA

For reading levels and more information, look up this title at www.lernerbooks.com.

Designed by Lindsey Owens.
Main body text set in Aptifer Sans LT Pro. Typeface provided by Linotype AG.
The illustrations in this book were created with Photoshop.

Library of Congress Cataloging-in-Publication Data

Names: Paul, Miranda, author. | Hong, Sija, illustrator.
Title: Beyond : discoveries from the outer reaches of space / Miranda Paul ; illustrated by Sija Hong.
Description: Minneapolis, MN : Millbrook Press, [2021] | Includes bibliographical references. | Audience:
    Ages 5–9 | Audience: Grades 2–3 | Summary: "Venture far beyond our solar system and discover the
    marvels of interstellar space. A wonder-filled poem and spectacular illustrations explore everything
    from dwarf planets and black holes to dark matter and brand-new stars" —Provided by publisher.
Identifiers: LCCN 2020014982 (print) | LCCN 2020014983 (ebook) | ISBN 9781541577565 (trade
    hardcover) | ISBN 9781728418988 (ebook)
Subjects: LCSH: Astronomy—Juvenile literature.
Classification: LCC QB46 .P385 2021 (print) | LCC QB46 (ebook) | DDC 520—dc23

LC record available at https://lccn.loc.gov/2020014982
LC ebook record available at https://lccn.loc.gov/2020014983

Manufactured in the United States of America
1-46779-47770-8/7/2020